COVER: **TWO CHILDREN**

1952   OIL, ARTIST'S COLLECTION

ON THE COVER PICASSO HELPS US TO
UNDERSTAND WHAT HE HAS SEEN AND
FELT. HE HAS DRAWN THE BOY AND
THE GIRL WITH SIMPLE LINES AND BRIGHT COLORS JUST
AS CHILDREN PAINT.

IF WE LET OUR EYES FOLLOW THE OUTLINES OF THE
TWO CHILDREN, WE FORM A LARGE CIRCLE AROUND
THEM. WITHIN THAT CIRCLE OUR ATTENTION MOVES
FROM THE BOY'S HEAD DOWN HIS CHEST AND ALONG
HIS ARM. HIS DRAWING HAND POINTS TO THE GIRL'S
HANDS, THEN UP THE CENTER
OF HER BODY
TO HER FACE.

HEAD OF A FAUN   1948

Permission SPADEM, 1969, by FRENCH REPRODUCTION RIGHTS INC.

WORLD RIGHTS RESERVED BY ERNEST RABOFF AND GEMINI-SMITH, INC.   ISBN Trade: 0-385-04924-2
                                                                  Library: 0-385-05115-8
LIBRARY OF CONGRESS CATALOG CARD NO. 68-26551   PRINTED IN JAPAN BY TOPPAN

HARLEQUIN ON HORSEBACK THE NATIONAL GALLERY, WASHINGTON D.C.

PABLO PICASSO

By Ernest Raboff

ART
FOR
CHILDREN

A GEMINI-SMITH BOOK

EDITED BY BRADLEY SMITH

PUBLISHED BY
DOUBLEDAY & CO., INC.

GARDEN CITY, NEW YORK
1968

PABLO PICASSO SAID:

"TO DRAW YOU MUST CLOSE YOUR EYES AND SING."

"THE WORK THAT ONE DOES IS ANOTHER WAY OF KEEPING A DIARY."

"I DO NOT SEEK, I FIND."

"I DON'T WORK AFTER NATURE, BUT BEFORE NATURE AND WITH HER."

"YOU CANNOT GO AGAINST NATURE. SHE IS STRONGER THAN THE STRONGEST MAN."

"IT IS NOT WHAT AN ARTIST DOES THAT COUNTS —BUT WHAT HE IS."

Picasso

DRAWINGS
OF PICASSO AT 26 AND AT 71 YEARS OF AGE — BY RABOFF

PABLO PICASSO (RUIZ) WAS BORN IN MALAGA, SPAIN, ON THE 25ᵀᴴ DAY OF OCTOBER, 1881.

HIS FATHER, JOSE RUIZ, WAS A PAINTER AND ART TEACHER.

MARIA PICASSO RUIZ WAS THE ARTIST'S MOTHER. SHE WAS KNOWN FOR HER WIT, SENSITIVITY AND INTELLIGENCE.

PABLO PICASSO'S MANY GIFTS INCLUDED:

EYES THAT SAW EVERYTHING, A **HEART** THAT LOVED ALL OF LIFE AND NATURE, **HANDS** THAT COULD CREATE GREAT WORKS OF ART.

SELF-PORTRAIT 1906

A.E. GALLATIN COLLECTION, PHILADELPHIA MUSEUM OF ART

"THE GOURMET" IS AN EARLY PICTURE PAINTED WHEN PICASSO WAS TWENTY YEARS OLD. FOR THE NEXT THREE YEARS HE USED LOTS OF BLUE PAINT ON HIS PALETTE, WHICH IS WHY THIS IS CALLED HIS "BLUE PERIOD." A WARM BLUE LIGHT IS SEEN IN ALL HIS PAINTINGS MADE AT THIS TIME.

A GOURMET IS A PERSON WHO LIKES GOOD FOOD. IN THIS PICTURE A LITTLE GIRL SCRAPES THE BOTTOM OF HER BOWL. THE LINES OF HER HAIR, THE FOLDS OF NAPKIN AROUND HER THROAT, ACROSS HER SHOULDER AND DOWN HER BACK, KEEP OUR EYES MOVING.

THE CIRCLE FORMED BY THE HEAD IS REPEATED BY THE POSITION OF HER ARMS, THE BOWL, THE TOP AND BOTTOM OF THE TABLECLOTH, AND THE HEM OF HER DRESS.

EVEN THE LINES OF THE FLOOR AND CURTAINS GIVE LIFE AND MOVEMENT TO THE PAINTING.

THE GOURMET   1901   OIL, CHESTER DALE COLLECTION, NEW YORK

"TWO SALTIMBANQUES WITH DOG" WAS PAINTED WHEN PICASSO'S
BLUE PERIOD WAS CHANGING INTO HIS ROSE PERIOD. THIS
CHANGE CAME AFTER HE MOVED FROM SPAIN TO FRANCE.
THE SOFT BLUE AND THE PALE PINK OF THESE PERIODS ARE
COMBINED HERE.

SALTIMBANQUES WERE MEN, WOMEN, GIRLS, AND BOYS WHO
FILLED MANY JOBS IN THE CIRCUS.

HERE, THE LARGER BOY WEARS A HARLEQUIN'S COSTUME.
THE YOUNGER ONE HAS ON AN ACROBAT'S SUIT.

THE TWO BOYS AND THE DOG ARE PAINTED STANDING CLOSE
TOGETHER. THEY WORK AND PLAY AND GO HOME WITH EACH
OTHER. THEY MUST BE GOOD FRIENDS. THEY EVEN LOOK
ALIKE. THEY MIGHT BE BROTHERS.

NOTICE HOW THE ARTIST MAKES A TALL AND A SHORT
BUILDING IN THE BACKGROUND TO MATCH THE TWO BOYS,
AND HOW THE
CLOUDS AND
SKY AND GROUND
CATCH THE ROSE
RAYS OF THE
SETTING SUN.

CIRCUS   1947, LITHOGRAPH

TWO SALTIMBANQUES WITH DOG ,   1905   COLLECTION OF MR. AND MRS. WILLIAM A. M. BURDEN, NEW YORK

"YOUNG GIRL ON A BALL" IS A PICTURE FULL OF FLOWING MOVEMENT. THE GIRL'S ARMS AND THE LINES OF HER BODY ARE PERFECTLY BALANCED ON THE BALL.

SEE HOW INTENT HER TRAINER IS — HE SEEMS READY TO CORRECT OR HELP HIS YOUNG PUPIL.

A MOTHER WITH A BABY ON HER SHOULDER WALKS IN THE DISTANCE WITH A CHILD AND A DOG.

AS PART OF THE PICTURE'S COMPOSITION, A WHITE HORSE FILLS THE SPACE BETWEEN THE ATHLETIC TRAINER AND THE BALANCING GIRL.

PICASSO PAINTED MANY PICTURES OF CIRCUS PEOPLE WHO WERE HIS FRIENDS AS WELL AS HIS MODELS.

HE PAINTED THIS PICTURE WHEN HE WAS TWENTY FOUR YEARS OLD.

FAMILY WITH MONKEY   1905

YOUNG GIRL ON A BALL   1905   THE LENINGRAD MUSEUM, MOSCOW

PICASSO PAINTED "BOWL OF FRUIT AND LOAVES ON A TABLE"
IN THE CUBIST STYLE.

CUBISM ATTEMPTED TO SHOW ON THE FLAT SURFACE OF
A CANVAS HOW MUCH SPACE AN OBJECT, LIKE A TABLE,
REALLY FILLED.

TO ILLUSTRATE THIS, THE FIRST DRAWING BELOW IS OF
THE TABLE AS IT WOULD ORDINARILY BE PAINTED.

IN CUBISM, PICASSO PAINTED IN THE TOP OF THE TABLE
AND THE SIDES OF THE LEGS ALSO, TO FILL THE SPACE
IN THE PAINTING JUST THE WAY THE TABLE FILLED THE
SPACE IN HIS ROOM, AS IS SUGGESTED BY THE SECOND
DRAWING.

THE LOAVES OF BREAD AND THE CURTAINS HAVE BEEN
SPREAD OUT, OR "CUBED" IN THE SAME WAY IN THIS
PAINTING.

PICASSO PAINTS IN MANY DIFFERENT STYLES BUT,
SINCE 1907, HE HAS OFTEN RETURNED TO CUBISM.

BOWL OF FRUIT AND LOAVES ON A TABLE   1908   OIL , KUNST MUSEUM , BASEL

THE "THREE MUSICIANS" ARE

A HARLEQUIN

A PIERROT

AND A MONK.

THE HARLEQUIN AND THE PIERROT
ARE FRENCH CLOWNS WHO NEVER
SPEAK WHILE THEY PERFORM. THE
MONK IS A QUIET RELIGIOUS MAN.

THE FIRST HOLDS A VIOLIN UNDER
HIS CHIN AND A BOW IN HIS HAND
ON THE TABLE. HE IS SEATED ON
OUR LEFT. IN THE CENTER, THE
PIERROT PLAYS THE CLARINET. ON

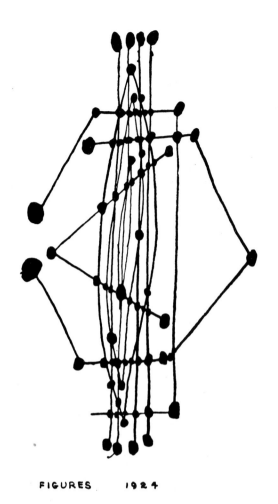

FIGURES 1924

THE RIGHT, THE MONK HAS AN ACCORDION. A MUSIC BOOK
IS LYING ON THE END OF THE TABLE IN FRONT OF THE
PIERROT'S CLARINET.

WE CAN SEPARATE PICASSO'S THREE MUSICIANS BY
THE COLORS AND DESIGNS OF THEIR COSTUMES.
THE HARLEQUIN IS IN ORANGE AND YELLOW, THE PIERROT IS
IN WHITE AND THE MONK IS WEARING A BROWN ROBE WITH
A WHITE ROPE BELT. PICASSO USES THE COLOR
AROUND THEM TO MAKE THE FIGURES EASIER TO SEE AND,
ALSO TO TIE THEM TOGETHER AS WE LOOK AT THE PICTURE.

THREE MUSICIANS   1921   OIL, PHILADELPHIA MUSEUM OF ART, A.E. GALLATIN COLLECTION

"MOTHER AND CHILD" IS A SUBJECT PICASSO HAS PAINTED
MANY TIMES. THIS ONE IS FROM HIS CLASSICAL PERIOD
WHICH BEGAN AROUND 1921 AND ENDED ABOUT 1927.

THE MOTHER AND CHILD ARE SEATED IN A CHAIR. THEY SEEM
TO BE CARVED OUT OF MARBLE.

THE COLORS ARE RICH AND WARM. IN THIS CLASSICAL
STYLE, PICASSO PAINTS SHAPES THAT ARE SOFT AND ROUND.
IN CUBISM, THEY WERE HARD AND SQUARE.

HIS CLASSICAL PERIOD PROBABLY WAS INSPIRED BY
THE DIGNITY AND BEAUTY OF THE ANCIENT GREEK AND
ROMAN SCULPTURE WHICH HE SAW ON A TRIP TO ITALY
IN 1917.

MOTHER AND CHILD   1922   OIL, A. HILLMAN COLLECTION, NEW YORK

THIS PAINTING OF "PAUL, SON OF THE ARTIST" IS AN
IMPORTANT CLASSICAL PERIOD WORK. PICASSO
FILLS THE PICTURE'S SPACE WITH THE BOY AND THE
DONKEY LIKE A DIAMOND SET IN A BRILLIANT
LANDSCAPE.

NOTICE HOW FIRMLY PAUL SITS IN THE SADDLE.
HE IS RELAXED AND SECURE. THE DONKEY SEEMS
TO BE GENTLE AND PATIENT. HE IS THE PERFECT
SIZE FOR HIS YOUNG RIDER. THEY MAKE A
FINE TEAM.

PICASSO HAS USED THE SAME BRUSHSTROKES FOR
THE HAIR OF THE ANIMAL AND THE GRASS OF
THE LAWN. IN THIS WAY
HE WEAVES TOGETHER
THE BACKGROUND AND THE
BOY ON HIS DONKEY.

FOR THE PAINTER, EACH
BRUSHSTROKE HAS AS MUCH
PURPOSE AND MEANING AS A
NOTE OF MUSIC DOES TO THE
COMPOSER.

PAUL, SON OF THE ARTIST   1923   COLLECTION OF THE ARTIST

"THE ROOSTER" HAS EYES THAT ROLL AROUND IN THEIR SOCKETS. WHEN HE CROWS, THEY BULGE FROM HIS HEAD, AND HIS TONGUE STICKS OUT.

HIS TAIL IS RAISED LIKE A BULLFIGHTER'S CAPE AND HE LOOKS READY TO CHALLENGE EVERY OTHER ANIMAL WHO MAY BE NEAR HIM.

HIS CHEST PUFFS OUT LIKE A SAIL FULL OF WIND. THE SPURS ON HIS LEGS ARE SHARP AS KNIVES.

HIS STRONG FEET ARE PLANTED FIRMLY ON THE GROUND.

PICASSO'S BIRD IS
KING OF THE ROOST.

TRIUMPH OF THE DOVE

THE ROOSTER , 1938   PASTEL   EX-COLLECTION F. PERLS , LOS ANGELES

PICASSO IS FAMOUS ALSO AS A FINE
SCULPTOR

HIS WORK "THE JESTER" WAS CREATED WHEN THE ARTIST WAS TWENTY-FIVE YEARS OLD.

WE FIND IN THIS SCULPTURE THE SAME UNDERSTANDING FOR CIRCUS PERFORMERS THAT WE DISCOVERED IN THE CIRCUS PAINTINGS OF HIS ROSE AND BLUE PERIODS.

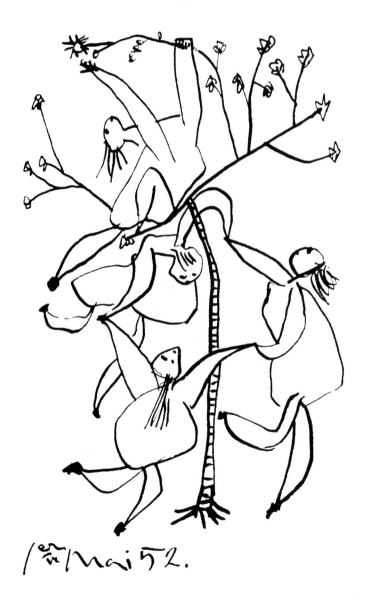

"THE JESTER" IS THE STUDY OF A MAN WHOSE JOB IT IS TO MAKE US LAUGH. IT IS A DIFFICULT AND NOBLE PROFESSION.

THE MAN'S JAW AND HIS EYES SHOW STRENGTH AND INTELLIGENCE.

PICASSO'S MASTERY OF THE SCULPTURE'S METAL IS SEEN IN THE HAT. IT SEEMS AS THOUGH IT WOULD BE SOFT AS CLOTH TO OUR TOUCH.

THE JESTER , BRONZE SCULPTURE   THE PHILLIPS GALLERY , WASHINGTON D.C.

PICASSO'S "PITCHER WITH FLOWERS" IS A
GRACEFUL, COLORFUL PICTURE. THE WORK CONTRASTS
AND BALANCES LINE AND COLOR WITH FORM.

THE BOWL OF FRUIT ON THE LEFT HAS THE CHARM
AND GAIETY OF A YOUNG GIRL DANCING IN A
BREEZE. THIS FEELING IS CREATED BY THE USE
OF SIMPLE LINES AND COLOR.

ON THE RIGHT, THE PITCHER STANDS LIKE A PROUD
MAN, WATCHING AND READY TO JOIN THE DANCE.
THE FLOWERS STICK UP LIKE FEATHERS IN A CAP.

THE LINE OF THE TABLETOP, THE TWO SMALL
PATCHES OF GREEN, AND THE CURVING AREAS OF
BLUE JOIN THEM TOGETHER IN HARMONY.

FIGURES FROM A SKETCHBOOK

PITCHER WITH FLOWERS   1937   W.W. CROCKER COLLECTION, SAN FRANCISCO MUSEUM OF ART

"MANDOLIN AND GUITAR" IS A STUDY IN CURVING LINES, MOVEMENT, AND BRILLIANT COLOR.

ON THE LEFT SIDE OF THE PAINTING, THE MANDOLIN IS SPREAD OUT IN SPACE. BOTH THE FLAT TOP AND THE ROUND BOTTOM SHOW THE TRUE FORM OF THE INSTRUMENT.

THE GUITAR IS PLACED ACROSS THE TABLE. WE CAN CLEARLY SEE ITS TOP AND SIDES.

BETWEEN THE MANDOLIN AND THE GUITAR STANDS A SCULPTURE SHAPED LIKE A GIRAFFE.

PICASSO KEEPS OUR EYES EXPLORING THE CANVAS BY REPEATING THE DESIGNS IN THE TABLECLOTH, ON THE WALLPAPER, THE SLANTED ROOF, IN THE BALCONY RAILINGS, AND ON THE WOODWORK UNDER THE TABLE.

THE OWL, 1946   LEAD-PENCIL

HE REPEATS THE COLORS IN THE SAME WAY, AND FOR THE SAME REASON.

WE EXPLORE EVERY DETAIL.

MANDOLIN AND GUITAR   1924   OIL WITH SAND   SOLOMON R. GUGGENHEIM MUSEUM , NEW YORK

"NIGHT FISHING AT ANTIBES" HAS THE SAME POWERFUL HONESTY AND DIRECT USE OF LINE THAT WE FIND IN CHILDREN'S DRAWINGS.

WITH GREAT SKILL, PICASSO HAS CAPTURED THE STRENGTH AND INTEREST OF THIS OLD, PRIMITIVE WAY OF FISHING. HE HAS USED THE POETRY OF FORM AND COLOR TO PAINT A MASTERFUL PICTURE.

BESIDES THE FISHERMEN WITH THEIR BOATS LANTERNS AND SPEARS, THE MOON AND THE BUILDINGS, WE SEE THE SPECTATORS AND EVEN MOTHS, CRABS, AND BIRDS.

PABLO PICASSO

PAINTER HISTORIAN SCULPTOR FATHER
POET   SCHOLAR   HUSBAND

IS ONE OF THE GREATEST ARTISTS OF ALL TIME.

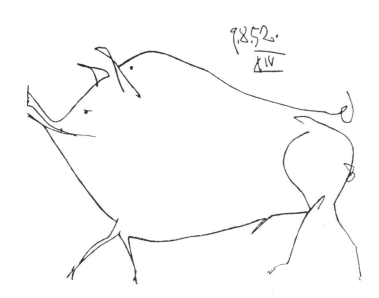

NIGHT FISHING AT ANTIBES   1939   THE MUSEUM OF MODERN ART, NEW YORK